D1571774

Odysseus's Odyssey

PREFACE

Out of all the stories in human history, "Homer's Odyssey, ancient Greece's most well-known epic poem, is officially the most influential story to have shaped the entire world, according to a poll of more than 100 international authors, academics, journalists, and critics conducted by Britain's BBC. The poll "100 Stories that Shaped the World," the British Broadcasting Corporation conducted in 2018 managed to show to the entire world how this marvelous epic creation of Homer keeps influencing generation upon generation."*

The 15 villanelles in this book of "Odysseus's Odyssey" are intended to capture the essence of the 15 adventures Odysseus encountered after he left Troy. The dialogue and solidarity are beyond what a 19 line villanelle could encompass. However, the poems may trigger your deeper fascination and intrigue your enthrallment of his pursuit.

Everyone's journey is his or her own Odyssey. In addition to Odysseus, many characters surfaced in this book: Robert Frost, John Milton, Edvard Munch, André Breton, Joseph of Egypt, Joseph of Nazareth, Joseph of Arimathea, William Shakespeare, Langston Hughes, Louise Bogan, Alexander the Great, Henry

Wadsworth Longfellow, T. S. Eliot, Anne Sexton, Gertrude Stein, James Wright, Walt Whitman, John Muir, Emily Dickinson and Rainer Maria Rilke. You will find a brief highlight of their lives, a poem about their odyssey, a particular image, glance, angle, perception...or simply, a poem dedicated to them.

At the end, Odysseus landed at Ithaca, strung his bow, returned home to reunite with his wife, Penelope, and his son, Telemachus. Some 3,300 years later, there is no difference; we sail and journey towards our destination, battle through our own odyssey, and in the end, we are all looking to return home and rest our souls.

*"Odyssey: Homer's Epic Poem Is Officially the World's Most Influential Story." An article reported by Nick Kampouris, published 4/4/21 in the "Greek Reporter."

Poetry Books by Livingston Rossmoor*

A Stream Keeps Running

Do You Hear What I Sing

A Journey in the Animal Kingdom

A Never-Ending Battle

When Ruby Was Still in My Arms

I Hear the Ocean Landing

The Thunder Was So Mad

I Found Ruth Tonight

Collected Triplets

Selected Ballads, Villanelles, Couplets,
Tanka Sequences, Cinquains & Triplets

Selected Sonnets

Selected Poems 2002-2017

Heart's Thread

Persephone's Spring

Rumi Inspiration

Odysseus's Odyssey

*For details, please visit www.livingstonrossmoor.com

Also by Livingston Rossmoor

Old Buddy Chang
(13 short stories)

One Ray of Light at Dawn
(Poetry & prose)

DVD & CD-One Ray of Light at Dawn
(11 Lyrics & Melodies)

One Ray of Light at Dawn
(Book of Music Scores)

The Beauty and the Ugly
(Poetry & prose)

DVD-Perpetual Stream
(10 Lyrics & Melodies)

Perpetual Stream
(Book of Music Scores)

Odysseus's Odyssey

Poems by Livingston Rossmoor

Published by
EGW Publishing
(Since 1979)

I dedicate this book to:
Scarlet Shinkle, Max Shinkle, Miles Shinkle,
Sullivan Lin, Bowie Lin, Lincoln Sandler,
Leo Sandler and Ruby Sandler.

Thanks to Lisa Rigge, Charles Sandler,
Andy Shinkle and Chris Slaughter for
reviewing this book. I also wish to thank
Chris Slaughter for the organization
and production of this book.

EGW Publishing (since 1979)

ISBN: 978-0-916393-50-2

www.livingstonrossmoor.com

I am indebted to the editors who published my poems:

"Moonlight" was published in *California Quarterly* (California State
Poetry Society), Summer 2021.

"Paradise" was published in *Chronogram* magazine, July 2021.

"Good luck to you, even so. Farewell! But if you only knew, down deep, what pains are fated to fill your cup before you reach that shore."

Homer

"But you, brave and adept from this day on . . . there's hope that you will reach your goal . . . the journey that stirs you now is not far off."

Homer

TABLE OF CONTENTS

CHAPTER I

Ismarus

Homebound from Troy, Ismarus is on his way.
Booty, plunder, killing Cicones was a cinch.
Quit, flee wasn't easy, Odysseus urged; sighed in dismay.

Cicones sought out Cicones, regrouped in a day.
Mellow wine, roasted sheep; here comes the grinch.
Home bound from Troy, Ismarus is on his way.

Swill, feast, crews rather get drunk and stay.
But no, not this time, Cicones will not flinch.
Quit, flee wasn't easy, Odysseus urged; sighed in dismay.

War is over, no rein, nothing keeps them at bay.
Pleasure is the king, not one death or lynch.
Home bound from Troy, Ismarus is on his way.

Chariots, soldiers, fierce force to make them pay.
Cicones fought back, gave them not an inch.
Quit, flee wasn't easy, Odysseus urged; sighed in dismay.

Odysseus was right, they should not linger and play.
Defeated, rowed away, escaped in a severe pinch.
Home bound from Troy, Ismarus is on his way.
Quit, flee wasn't easy, Odysseus urged; sighed in dismay.

Land of the Lotus-Eaters

The ships plunged headlong in the howling gale.
Off course nine whole days, lost in the deadly sea.
Land of the Lotus-eaters, hearty and hale.

Squadron reached the shore with rags of sail.
Odysseus dispatched runners to scout and see.
The ships landed in the howling gale.

Flowers, fragrance, everyone is happy, no one wails.
They eat lotus; fruit and flower, kind and glee.
Land of the Lotus-eaters, hearty and hale.

None slain, they feed crew lotus from ponds in the dale.
A heavenly fruit? That's why none return or flee?
The ships landed in the howling gale.

Smirk, daze, dazzle; can't remember head or tail?
All desires gone, grazing on lotus, relaxed and free.
Land of the Lotus-eaters, hearty and hale.

Forgetting the journey home, memory fails.
Odysseus, the sole one can still hear and speak.
The ships plunged headlong in the howling gale.
Land of the Lotus-eaters, hearty and hale.

The Cyclops Owns His Cave

A Nobody would have escaped Cyclops's chase.
Blinded Polyphemus screams to hunt him down.
Odysseus boasts and taunts, leaves a trace.

Odysseus isn't afraid to fight back, he's a champ, an ace.
Each Cyclops owns his cave; there's no village or town.
A Nobody would have escaped Cyclops's chase.

Polyphemus, a giant cannibal, one eye, big face,
limb from limb, rips and smushes prey down.
Odysseus boasts and taunts, leaves a trace.

Polyphemus fears not Zeus, no respect, no grace,
gulps down flesh and barks: "You are a fool,"*
a Nobody would have escaped Cyclops's chase.

Devours two men to sate his hunger, a weird pace.
In sleep, hero stabs monster's eye below his crown,
Odysseus boasts and taunts, leaves a trace.

Poseidon, monster's father, furious about this disgrace,
riled the beast, blinded his son, doomed to drift and drown.
A Nobody would have escaped Cyclops's chase.
Odysseus boasts and taunts, leaves a trace.

*From the poem "Odyssey," by Homer.

Aeolus, the God of the Winds

Aeolus captured all adverse winds in a sack.
Nine days smooth sailing, Odysseus fell asleep.
His men loosened the bag, completely on the wrong track.

Odysseus, the story teller, keeps Aeolus on track
about brute battle of Troy; trembles, gloats and weeps.
Aeolus captured all adverse winds in a sack.

The wind god set west winds free to blow them back.
Aeolus fastened the sack so tight, no puff can seep.
His men loosened the bag, completely on the wrong track.

They see their natives tending fires and crops in stacks.
But what's in the sack? Crews mutter, grumble and cheep.
Aeolus captured all adverse winds in a sack.

Never go home empty-handed, they took a crack,
glanced each other, "Treasure trove must be deep?"
His men loosened the bag, completely on the wrong track.

A moment of greed, sudden squalls burst out, back, back,
thwacked them all the way back, toll is very steep.
Aeolus captured all adverse winds in a sack.
His men loosened the bag, completely on the wrong track.

Laestrygonian

Odysseus begged, Aeolus refused, no more.
Eat your own mistakes. "Out," he shouts, "get out!"
Row, row, 7 days to Laestrygonian land, oar by oar.

Who lives here? Men live on bread? Beast? Boar?
Three men were sent to probe the land and scout.
Odysseus begged, Aeolus refused. No more.

Like a mountain crag, from ceiling to floor,
she summons her husband, huge and stout.
Row, row, 7 days to Laestrygonian land, oar by oar.

He tears one up for dinner, shakes to the core,
two flee, run for lives; not just bully or clout.
Odysseus begged, Aeolus refused. No more.

Hundreds join the strike after the howl and roar.
They spear, pierce men like fish, a complete rout.
Row, row, 7 days to Laestrygonian land, oar by oar.

Rocks shatter hulls, save one, all gone: fleet and corps.
Crews should've kept winds in the sack with no doubt.
Odysseus begged, Aeolus refused. No more.
Row, row, 7 days to Laestrygonian land, oar by oar.

CHAPTER II

Circe's Island of Aeaea

Perils, crises, more to come before they die.
The home of Circe, the nymph with lovely braids.
Circe's wand turned them all into swine in a sty.

Spellbinding voice, potion to shut every eye,
any thoughts of going home vanish and fade.
Perils, crises, more to come before they die.

Groink, groink, this is how they grunt and cry.
Hermès shed light to get Odysseus out of ploy.
Circe's wand turned them all into swine in a sty.

A magic herb to fend off potion's high,
shields and counters the wand by sword and blade.
Perils, crises, more to come before they die.

For one year, feast and wine, crews started to pry.
Home? What good are all these jades and maids?
Circe's wand turned them all into swine in a sty.

Keeping her words, Circe succumbed to their cries.
But, first to House of Death to ask for Tiresias's aid.
Perils, crises, more to come before they die.
Circe's wand turned them all into swine in a sty.

Agamemnon at the Kingdom of the Dead

Odysseus meets Agamemnon at the kingdom of the dead.
Shrill with grief, tears spring to his eyes, he sighs.
What a heinous plot, no pity, not a shred.

Greek king of Trojan War, he chopped countless heads.
But, set-up by his wife, a wretched death, he dies.
Odysseus meets Agamemnon at the kingdom of the dead.

Clytemnestra schemed his death; vicious, dread;
while he fought ten-year war after bidding her good-bye.
What a heinous plot, no pity, not a shred.

Aegisthus feasted him, sealed the hall, no one fled.
And Cassandra, Agamemnon's wife's death-cry.
Odysseus meets Agamemnon at the kingdom of the dead.

She turned her back on him; while he's dying, bled and bled,
even lacked the heart to close his jaws, seal his eyes.
What a heinous plot, no pity, not a shred.

A warning, trust no one in the same bed,
Agamemnon's ghost pressing on, keeps asking why?
Odysseus meets Agamemnon at the kingdom of the dead.
What a heinous plot, no pity, not a shred.

Sirens

Circe keeps her promises, gifts foresight.
Withered, wrinkled skin like rags on their bones,
rotten to death, when sirens enchant, a sorry plight.

Back from House of Death alive, what a rite.
Odysseus doomed to die twice, forever in groan.
Circe keeps her promises, gifts foresight.

This time, Odysseus informs crew to join the fight.
Soften beeswax, seal ears, hear nothing, none.
Rotten to death, when sirens enchant, a sorry plight.

Circe knows Odysseus thirsts to take the bite,
hear the sirens, his curious mind is beyond well known.
Circe keeps her promises, gifts foresight.

He asked crews to tie him up, at the height
of ravishing voice, rope over rope, ignore his moan.
Rotten to death, when sirens enchant, a sorry plight.

Hard, harder, row past sirens, it's a dire fright.
Next, two monsters, no place deadlier than that zone.
Circe keeps her promises, gifts foresight.
Rotten to death, when sirens enchant, a sorry plight.

Scylla and Charybdis

With Circe's advice, Odysseus set his goal.
Don't fight back, escape, let Scylla attain her aim.
Six hideous heads, six long swaying necks, no soul.

Steers past Charybdis, dodges ruining the whole.
Charybdis gulps and spews everything, lays her claim.
With Circe's advice, Odysseus set his goal.

Scylla's fangs in each head snaps one man for her toll.
Hands, feet hoisted over Odysseus's head, calling his name.
Six hideous heads, six long swaying necks, no soul.

Swung up the cliff; screaming with bloody cheek and jowl,
she bolts them down, into cavern, smushes and maims.
With Circe's advice, Odysseus set his goal.

This wrenched his heart the most among all death scroll
through all tearful things: crime, pity, shame and blame.
Six hideous heads, six long swaying necks, no soul.

Putting two behemoths astern, he ducks the hole.
Fight not Charybdis's whirlpool, a feat, not a shame.
With Circe's advice, Odysseus set his goal.
Six hideous heads, six long swaying necks, no soul.

Helios, the Sun God

Killing herds, dear price paid, let things be.
Handsome cattle, cherished by Helios up there.
Circe, Tiresias warn and warn, a stern plea.

A woeful prophecy, Tiresias never lies.
If violated, dire, doom, no one will be spared.
Killing herds, dear price paid, let things be.

Escape from Scylla, Charybdis, and flee,
exhausted crew begged to land, rest in peace with no scare.
Circe, Tiresias warn and warn, a stern plea.

Swore the oath, hands off, leave herds mellow with glee.
Stalled for one month, only wrong winds in the air.
Killing herds, dear price paid, let things be.

Supplies scarce, hunger drove them inland to hunt and see.
Starving, falling asleep; crews made the kill, they dare!
Circe, Tiresias warn and warn, a stern plea.

Helios bursts, Zeus grants their deaths, kill them at sea.
Lightning strikes, hulls into splinters, rip and tear.
Killing herds, dear price paid, let things be.
Circe, Tiresias warn and warn, a stern plea.

CHAPTER III

Ogygia, Calypso's Island

All gone, all dead, all his men, all and all.
Only he bore the lightning bolt and thunder.
Ogygia, Calypso's island, a seven-year thrall.

Riding makeshift raft, nine-days drift, drag and crawl,
he survived, a miracle to reach the shore.
All gone, all dead, all his men, all and all.

Escaping from Helios, the island of Sol,
Calypso takes him, loves him to the core,
Ogygia, Calypso's island, a seven-year thrall.

Odysseus craves to go home, waits for the call,
gazes at the sea; sobs, tears, grieves all the blunders.
All gone, all dead, all his men, all and all.

Athena convinced Zeus to free him from her pall.
She complies at the end, heartbreak to sunder.
Ogygia, Calypso's island, a seven-year thrall.

Ax, adze, she leads Odysseus to where trees grow tall,
he builds the boat in four days, what a wonder.
All gone, all dead, all his men, all and all.
Ogygia, Calypso's island, a seven-year thrall.

Island of Phaeacians

Lord of the Seas spies him sailing near Phaeacia's shore.
Who dared? Never let him get loose from snare of pain.
Who abetted? Poseidon's ire boils even more.

Stares, scans the stars, pursues whatever is in store,
Odysseus heeds Calypso's guide, narrows the lane.
Lord of the Seas spies him sailing near Phaeacia's shore.

Clouds, gales clash; waves, storms smash, Poseidon roars.
Doomed to die? He senses it in every pulse and vein.
Who abetted? Poseidon's ire boils even more.

Dives, swims, adrift two days two nights, sore and hoar,
he set foot on land again, where Alcinuous reigns.
Lord of the Seas spies him sailing near Phaeacia's shore.

Nausicaa, the princess, shows him queen's door
where the key to return home is lain.
Who abetted? Poseidon's ire boils even more.

A sailor running for his life, oar by oar,
once, fleet admiral, ship captain, glorious rein.
Lord of the Seas spies him sailing near Phaeacia's shore.
Who abetted? Poseidon's ire boils even more.

Ithaca at Last

The Earthshaker grabs the hand of Zeus,
punishes Odysseus, crushes him into tears of grief.
How can immortals lose battle, calling a truce?

Threat, trap, torture, torment not just bruise.
What a story! Not any tale out of a bag or sheaf.
The Earthshaker grabs the hand of Zeus.

Cry, cry for Odysseus, a hero, not a wuss.
Racing, racing, Poseidon's nap is brief.
How can immortals lose battle, calling a truce?

Through wars, shipwrecks, he endured every ruse.
Whizzing through the sea, Phaeacian's ship like a leaf.
The Earthshaker grabs the hand of Zeus.

No place, no wound, save the backbone and crus.
Ithaca at last, clear through hidden shoal and reef.
How can immortals lose battle, calling a truce?

Athena revives Odysseus's vigor and juice;
pride, keeping promises, foremost and chief.
The Earthshaker grabs the hand of Zeus.
How can immortals lose battle, calling a truce?

Odysseus, the Beggar

Athena disguised him as an old beggar, not brave.
No fire in his eyes, grungy, smudge and grime.
108 noblemen would maul him into his grave.

Feasted on his hogs, cows and sheep, these suitors, knaves,
swilled his best wine, day in day out on his dime.
Athena disguised him as an old beggar, not brave.

"Trust me, gods are on our side,"* don't cede or cave.
Odysseus and his son plot, plan, bide their time.
108 noblemen would maul them into their graves.

Penelope waits for him, longs and craves.
20 years in tears, day and night, wasted her prime.
Athena disguised him as an old beggar, not brave.

Fight them even if they impose, obtrude, enslave.
He swears to slay and end this farce and mime.
108 noblemen would maul them into their graves.

A restless night, before killing them all, none save.
He and his son prayed, let them pay for their crimes.
Athena disguised him as an old beggar, not brave.
108 noblemen would maul them into their graves.

*From the poem "Odyssey," by Homer.

Odysseus Strings His Bow

The moment is here, Odysseus strings his bow.
Suitors take their turns; pull, stretch, everyone fails.
She offered the contest for her wedding vow.

Penelope's suspicion of the beggar grows.
Odysseus back? Rumor, facts, so many tales.
The moment is here, Odysseus strings his bow.

Arrow through Antinous's throat, the world knows,
bloodshed is on, the king is back, truth unveils.
She offered the contest for her wedding vow.

He's here, he's back, "kill suitors and all,"* old nurse glows.
She asked if it could be, if God answered her decades of wails.
The moment is here, Odysseus strings his bow.

The scar, the secret of his bed, she heeds now,
years of belief, disbelief after he set sail.
She offered the contest for her wedding vow.

Falls to her knees, she flings her arms, lets tears flow.
Holds him tight, in hell, in heaven, hails in hale.
The moment is here, Odysseus strings his bow.
She offered the contest for her wedding vow.

*From the poem "Odyssey," by Homer.

CHAPTER IV

It Was Meant to Be
(for Robert Frost)

It was a day the whole world was watching.
"The Gift Outright" was read at JFK inauguration.
It was historical to invite Frost to recite the poem.
First time in history, poetry took the world stage.
A man of books and learning identified
the country with art and culture.
Sarcasm was silenced, humanity humbled.

Two years later, a eulogy by JFK for Frost, he expressed that
art is a form of truth, not propaganda.

Ten months later, "Stopping by Woods on a Snowy Evening"
was quoted at JFK's funeral.

JFK's voice, writings, ring aloud forever; power, arrogance,
poetry reminds our limitations; rotten, corrupt, let poetry
cleanse; prejudiced, biased, poetry expands our minds to
richness, brings us diverse views, ideas and perspectives...*
JFK's writing, on the wall, voice's still there.
A president, a prophet, a poet.

73

It was meant to be from the beginning.
Mental illness, depression: mother,
sister and you, and then, your wife, daughters and son.
It was meant for you to cling to the forest,
attach to the farm, the nature, the soil.
It was meant for you to live a long life for this invitation.
The day poetry sealed its kismet and shantih.

Drifting in the woods, no road to be taken.
Witness the dye-loaded wind coloring the leaves,
snowflakes arriving to brush the bare branches,
stare at the sprigs twitching in the gray sky.
Through the long cold nights, the day will come,
creeks gather morning dew, a gift from the sun.
Running water under the icy snow and sleet.
Horses neigh to rouse a new day, embark with first step
toward the miles and miles yet to go.

*Inspired by JFK's article in The Atlantic, February 1964.

I Am Coming Home
(for John Milton)

Once I was permitted to visit the garden.
I heard Satan's curses, angel's cry,
Charon's bouncing coins, and Hades on Satan's side,
the free fall of guilt, the knock in the midnight.
No eyes were blurred, no vision to be blocked.
And what's the use to deny the loss of sight?
Lament the world is coming to an end,
and pity the fall of man. Prophet was not I,
before the sunrise, I rose, I listened to
the Bible, walked in the forest, and birds' trill
brightened my day while rustling leaves pleased my ear.
I followed the voice, the calling.
I could not see the smile, the crying face,
the feigned gesture, the anger, the hatred,
the innocence of baby's eyes,
the peril if someone set a trap.
I could not see the world. The world saw me well.
Then God instructed me through my soul,
He cleansed my senses, my smell and hearing,
He polished my inward mirror,
reflecting the light dictating my verses.

My eyes blinded, my bond intact, my burden,
my duty, my faith and conscience remains.
The fall of Adam, the loss of Eve and Eden.
Stray, roam, woe, peace, I am coming home.

The Scream
(for Edvard Munch)

Scream.
Scream.
Scream.
We hear you.
Into those convoluted clouds.

Sometimes, the young and clear,
still believe there is a way,
calming down,
pace returns.
Sometimes, from a faded pining of a skeleton,
obsessing phantom collapsed by last straw of justice.
Sometimes, the guttural groan failed to crackle
the kindness of the memory.
Sometimes, the color painted so thick,
regardless the dissent,
the voice is dead,
the mercy of birth,
the only warmth.

Still, you painted us a bridge.
Clouds kept the scream.
Never dissipated.
All swathing up there:
Achilles, Agamemnon, Hector, Odysseus;
Aeneas, Dido.......Uriah the Hittite....
Light, hope, grace, caritas.
We scream.
"Ambitions, coveting, change of prides, disdain..."*
Posthumus screams.
"Blow, winds, and crack your cheeks! rage! blow!"**
Lear screams.

Roar, howl, louder, louder.
We hear you.

Prospero, Crusoe....screams, screams,
echoes of the barren island.

Strangle, smother,
deafening now.
You hear We,
don't you?

*From the play "Cymbeline," by William Shakespeare.
 **From the play "King Lear," by William Shakespeare.

Advice to the Next Prophet

It is finally coming to an end.
Someone likes to say,
"the end is the beginning,"
or "the beginning is the end."
But it means nothing to you,
there is no end.

You never stop questioning,
quarrels persist;
leaves bid good-bye,
sprigs divorce branches,
whatever left is being recognized.
The only reward,
immune to death like Tithonus?

Everything Is Naked
(for André Breton)

What else to want?
Sky is not blue **enough**?
The bird is too fleeting?

I always think if I stare long enough,
everything is naked.

Veer and roam,
without purpose,
is that good enough?
Hey deer,
does anyone hear?

Look at my eyes,
piercing bright,
who said,
intended not to stun.

Saytrs will never forgive us,
if we do not learn how to dance.

CHAPTER V

Moonlight*

You always foresee
the way to a tranquil life;
amble the sidewalks,
let the world pass by,
leave the war to the Olympians.
You still expect if you breathe, stare into the sky,
some stars will guide you.
You are right.
The path goes first through Asphodel meadows,
flowers under sun, still.

I try to answer your murmuring every night,
if you gaze harder,
angels will turn into stars.

*Published in *California Quarterly,*
California State Poetry Society, Summer 2021.

Joseph of Egypt

Ten brothers betrayed you.
Some said killed, some said sold.
Midianite merchants took you through
the desert to Egypt, a slave with tales untold.
From jail, your fate flourished, loud and bold.

Able were you, second to Pharaoh,
"How statue-like I see thee stand."*
The whole country was blessed by your hand!
Brain, faith were your sword and arrow.
For Moses, you sowed the fertile land.

Merciful were you, forgave brothers' evil deed,
saved the whole clan from famine and starvation.
Canaan to Goshen, you answered every need.
To the glory and sufferings, you built the nation.
For "Exodus,"** you planted the seed.

*"To Helen," poem by Edgar Allan Poe.
**Bible chapter.

Joseph of Nazareth

Husband of Mary, that was you.
Before marriage, "she was found to be
with child through the Holy Spirit,"* no clue,
bewildered in the dark, you must be.
Saved her from public disgrace, angel's plea.

You listened, and listened well.
A righteous man, everyone can see.
Magi's star, Herod's curse. "Get up...and flee,"**
angel's voice; "Run, run, keep quiet, don't yell."
Back from Egypt, "He will be called a Nazarene."***

For thirty years, room and board.
Childhood, teens, youth, under the same roof,
and time would come to cut the cord.
You knew, you knew, you never asked for proof,
the blessing was bestowed by the Lord.

*Bible, Matthew 1:18
**Bible, Matthew 2:13
***Bible, Matthew 2:23

Joseph of Arimathea

How you twisted the arms of Pilate,
before Pharisees maligned the gloom and doom.
A disciple of Jesus. He is your Pilot.
You took the body, placed it in your new tomb.
You saw the light out of darkness of the womb.

Witnessing his death, you acted fast,
wrapped the body in a clean linen cloth,
rolled a big stone, blocked the tomb, pledged your troth.
You went away and disappeared into the past,
as though what you did was nothing but the froth.

What if Pharisees got ahead of you?
Or Pilate did not grant you the body?
Or if no new tomb was ready, you knew
history would be a mess, rough and shoddy.
And you, just a shadow before the morning dew?

Peace

I heard you were looking for me.

In the early morning,
so quiet,
you can hear everything,
when turkeys and geese
exhausted their exchanges of last callings,
birds have not yet awakened.

You must hear something in that vast silence.
Yet you are still searching.
Didn't the rising sun show you the path?
Too bright, too dazzled?
And the heat at high noon is too hot?

You waited for me after sunset.
I saw you light a candle.
Advent? Hanukkah?
Or just for the long dark night,
so I can find you?

For the Rain to Rain, the Sun to Glow
(for William Shakespeare)

"When that I was and a little tiny boy,
With hey, ho, the wind and the rain;"* both blow,
To write or not is thornier than a ploy,
For the rain to rain, the sun to glow.

But when I grew and came to manhood,
With hey, ho, the wind and the rain;"* both blow,
With a knack to act and I who stood,
For the rain to rain, the sun to glow.

While drive my play to tie the knot to knot,
With hey, ho, the wind and the rain;"* both blow,
By rubbing salt in the wound, by wielding plot,
For the rain to rain, the sun to glow.

As Globe my theater that began to thrive,
With hey, ho, the wind and the rain;"* both blow,
With jealousy and spite, they cheer and jive,
For the rain to rain, the sun to glow.

But when the plague that swept my town,
With hey, ho, the wind never ceased to blow,
I wrote sonnets, poems as theater's down,
For the rain to rain, the sun to glow.

A glorious moment celebrated my fame,
With hey, ho, the wind never ceased to blow,
By juicing characters and spicing the game,
For the rain to rain, the sun to glow.

And I who reap the hay that play my hand,
With hey, ho, the wind never ceased to blow,
But that was fun as I created my brand,
For the rain to rain, the sun to glow.

But when I passed, my offspring those whom all died,
With hey, ho, the wind never ceased to blow,
Regrets, I did have some while life is but a glide.
For the rain to rain, the sun to glow.

*From the song "When that I was and a little tiny boy," and the play
"Twelfth Night," by William Shakespeare.

That Night

That night Heaven opened.
Candles led the way through
darkened skies.
The singing was quiet.
For every soul
the voice delivered the lesson;
gratification lingered,
echoed,
front to rear.
Upfront, there are several steps,
every step took us one step
closer to the gate that shines the light.

The night ended in
merciful silence.

Years after, we recall the voice,
singing, candles, harmony and serenity.

No one remembers the lesson.

CHAPTER VI

Instill the Pride
(for Langston Hughes)

Darkest night, narrowest alley.
Don't you ever turn back.
Acquaint the dimming street light.
Count the Dippers in the sky.
Head up, don't you droop.
No one owes you a dime.
Who cares your toes touch the earth.
Straighten your spine for pride to shine.

The Last Quartet
(for Louise Bogan)

Now that I wake up and see the sun rise, I run.
The dead are washed away as the sand
in a citadel; the gate closes, shadows stand;
search for a resting place, there are none.
Nest is being built, birds are born to fly.
Lift the veil that tangled in the gravity-pull,
wheel is spinning, kitten chasing the spool.
In the cocoon, another winter over cloudy sky.

Now that I wake up and see the sun rise, I run.

Now that the horizon surfaces, I see.
The light concealed the invisible trap.
Cascading streams lay out the map.
The course bends and contours into the sea.
It is the mountain answering the call.
Branches swerve, leaves shiver in the sneer
of relentless blow that silences the vestigial cheer.
In the quiet, rusted boat hauling the trawl.

Now that the horizon surfaces, I see.

Now that the storm passed, in the sunset, I walk.
The pace is deterred by the tempest-hail.
Calming draft breezes along the hidden trail.
Now, the flowers wave on top of the stalk;
Thunder flashes its warning to no avail.
The gap separates, the gorge stretches;
In the dream, the seized victim sketches
a path to ditch the agony of travail.

Now that the storm passed, in the sunset, I walk.

Now that I have the permission, I wait.
Magma chamber simmers in the hot air.
Smells, follow the hot stink to the fox's lair.
The moment of truth dictates my fate.
Salmon battle in the falls, strive upstream.
Saxifrage strains to split through the rocks,
must I call up Daemon to unlock the block?
Lava's marbled colors in a sizzling steam.

Now that I have the permission, I wait.

Alexander the Great

I carried "Iliad"* with me,
a gift from Aristotle.
No Achilles's heel, nor any knot,
like the one
between Achilles and Agamemnon.
Nothing stopped me,
I was born to conquer, Zeus saw it all.

I cut through every knot,
Phrygian knew it well,
no Gordian knot,
Nile to Indus, Oxus,
never shed a tear
except for my dear Bucephalus.

I died too young,
no time to tend your unresolved quests:
how many swords for endless knot of Samsara?
How many prayers in the knots of the Rosary?
Seen, unseen;
to cut, or not to cut?

*A poem by Homer.

Building a Life
(for Henry Wadsworth Longfellow)

Bypass the agony of defeat and woe,
stand on your own two feet,
wrestle and climb from the slough,
bitter or sweet, drum up the beat.

Tell me not to tremble and dither,
or fear the depth of the darkest pit.
Gallop before they all start to wither;
inch forward with temerity and grit.

With the hope that rides with the wind
and the light at dawn. The first ray
reveals its colors, brightens every mind,
refreshing morning dew, sparkles every day.

Breathe and taste the new air,
embrace the boon, bust and strife;
babies cry, sleep, smile and stare
at the unfolding wonder of life.

Architects of family builders.
Ardor and zeal are the proof.
Build the foundation, erect the pillars,
set the beam, secure the roof.

Day and night, strive and stride,
with love and drive,
a sense of duty and pride,
the audacity to live and thrive.

The challenge, afraid not;
a resolve to face it all,
overcome every bump and blot,
earnest soul answers every call.

Dive the deepest, fly the highest,
ski any mountain, surf every sea,
moment of truth is present; unbiased,
impartial, to be anything you can be.

The passing of baton, aging of body and soul.
A miracle, still in one piece.
Rekindle the fire, reset the goal
with humbling silence and peace.

The curse of setback and affliction.
In the gulch, cold and quiver;
breezes whisper, a hint, a conviction,
an uplifting clue to rive the shiver.

Blast of endless ravages, no place no scars.
Slander, odium, failure and outcry,
thwart us not to look at the stars
glimmering in the pitch-dark sky.

Scourge of tragedy, ordeal of
burnt-out bodies, shatterer of dreams,
pathos of wounded souls, forsaken love,
cease not the stream of celestial gleams.

The dire of debacle, burning beyond repair,
calamity of breakdown and injury,
anguish of injustice, sigh of despair,
adversity, misfortune, misery,
block not the perpetual shimmering light.
Sun will rise, wind will blow,
carrying us from the darkest night
to the morning glow.

Cookies Still Crumble

I can hear what you can't.
I can see what you can't.
Like tomorrow's sun, I will rise
a fresh shine.
You keep reminding me;
shadows, shadows.
But I hurl them behind me;
like trees, roses, lilies,
tulips, milkweed...
even impatiens lying on the ground,
in the shade;
shadows everywhere.

I live in a world you do not know.
Sun, light, umbra,
do not come into play,
flowers, trees, greens, mean nothing;

Cookies still crumble,
that's all we agree.

CHAPTER VII

You and I
(for T.S. Eliot)

No clouds to impede sun's penetration,
every corner,
icy, hot, brands of origin;
young and old, men, women, teenagers.
Something through air to the clouds is free to travel,
it silences every mouth, lowers
every head. No alcohol, no drug, no arrest.
A civilized addiction. People come, register
to the wire, reply, reply to the reply.
Nothing on the face; glue
to the Medusa screen.

In the nightfall,
you and I by the crowding sports bar.
A noisy group embraces the exuberant panache,
impels the clan to rip the roof,
unconciliatory,
no backing down, no drooping.
The souls are geared to make
a pungent and lasting scoop.
The bravery of the troop.

Near the window, a quiet couple.
Heads behind menu.
"The Equilibrists"* only transaction,
measure their minutes in the multiple barriers
of sound waves.

You and I, follow the usual daily grind,
chat and sip with regular frequency,
enough to boil the rather humdrum routine,
just adequate to cheer the
sapless souls in an insipid bind.

The gang rippled in the mundane causeries
and heated sarcasm,
double down to abide not the comity,
not a riddle or a burden to
abdicate urbanity.

You and I, alone in the corner,
filtering thick noises, bursts in the crowded air;
immersing in the dim light; a dream of predawn darkness,
encumbered with ominous foreboding,
a challenge to ride Plath's "Ariel." Do you dare?
Do I dare? Gallop above every stare.

*A poem by John Crowe Ransom.

The Tides Wash Away the Sand Castle
(for Anne Sexton)

Follow the lane, abide by the rule, I drive.
The searches begin with the rhythm; petrify
beneath the veneer. Hidden beats drum up
the blessings, foment the curse.
The tides wash away the sand castle.

Set the alarm, take the meds, I strive.
The train sounds its approval, bids good-bye.
The escalation keeps piling up,
it pauses, waits for the night to come, sun to rise.
The tides wash away the sand castle.

Solemnly with a moment of truth, I shrive.
Solid as a rock, never blinks an eye;
a wrong exchange ruptures all the build-up.
Dikes burst; floods over bank, a blight in disguise.
The tides wash away the sand castle.

Keeping my head above water, I swim and dive.
The thread is there till broken. I stand up to the pry;
a ludicrous query, the debate heats up,
a few misspelled words decimate the praise.
The tides wash away the sand castle.

The Trojan Horse

A beggar in Troy, begging from wall to hall.
Helen recognized him on the spot.
Yes, Odysseus held us back, saved us all.

Ripped and grimy, what is Odysseus's call?
Helen swore an oath, he revealed the plot.
A beggar in Troy, begging from wall to hall.

Steal Palladium, then Troy can be taken and fall.
Ten year war, wooden horse is the final lot.
Yes, Odysseus held us back, saved us all.

What a brazen plot, the horse stands tall.
Priam hauls it inside Troy, a sacred knot?
A beggar in Troy, begging from wall to hall.

Agamemnon's best encamped for the bloody death brawl.
Deiphobus courting Helen, boiling hot.
Yes, Odysseus held us back, saved us all.

Helen calls out each by name, we crouch and crawl.
Inside the horse's belly, he shut us still, tongues not.
A beggar in Troy, begging from wall to hall.
Yes, Odysseus held us back, saved us all.

The Button

Black sky, fierce waves, gusty gale,
wars, battles, departures, coming home,
a stormy journey.
Ulysses knew when and where
to push the button
to move earth and heaven.
Tennyson strived "to seek, to find,
and not to yield,"*
over the horizon
he just stared.

Grass all over Austerlitz and Waterloo.
Gettysburg's address ringing
a new birth of freedom in the air.
Sandburg knew the grass covers all,
at Verdun and Ypres.
Someone pushed the button.

For sure, grass grows at Auschwitz,
so does the passion
to read Anne Frank's diary.
Paper cranes for Sadako Sasaki
piled high at Hiroshima.
The button was pushed
with deliberate precision.

Same earth, same water as in Genesis.
Same polarization, same falling apart.
This time is different.
This road has never been taken.
After this button,
no more buttons.
All silence, nothing left.
No mail,
no tweet,
no grass will grow,
no places to hide the diary,
no hands to fold paper crane,
no horizon to stare.

*From the poem "Ulysses," by Alfred, Lord Tennyson.

When Are You Coming Home?
(for Gertrude Stein)

Your shadow behind you.
Your shadow greets you.

I just keep on rolling,
rolling in my circle.

The bus never comes.
The flag waves in the far distance.

Emerald City,
ruby red slippers,
the yellow brick road.

Can't you hear the tinkling?
Who is waiting for whom?
When are you coming home?

118

CHAPTER VIII

Pray
(for James Wright)

It never changes, shadow of the elder tree.
Under the clouds, it is dark,
keeping its silence.
And now.
The moon decides to show her face,
listens to every plea.
An old man raises his voice, a wolf's howling,
proclaims, resonates
in the hallowed emptiness.
Now the sound
dies in midair, then all disappears.
I hide behind the mound of after-harvest dry rice plants
near the barn,
keep breathing to myself,
I listen and stare,
scrutinize around,
along the stretch, scarecrows are all in tears.
I swivel to myself and swallow mine.

Work
(for Walt Whitman)

Work, out of bed, went to work at daybreak.
Work, all I can remember, while others went to school.
Work, meager living, got hands dirty.
Work, printing, typesetting, editing, publishing.
Work, self-taught, written word became my love.
Work, just me and my "Leaves of Grass."*
Work, with wounded soldiers.
Work, spoke out for peace and war.
Work, spoke out for the country.
Work, spoke out for the land, the soil.
Work, spoke out for every leaf, every blade of grass.
Work, the fair, the ugly, the foul.
Work, a voice for the young and old.
Work, repeat, relentless to reach the soul.
Work, I breathe, I die.

*A book by Walt Whitman.

John of the Mountains
(for John Muir, also known as "John of the Mountains")

John of the Mountains rose up in his youth,
wandered the coastline and the countryside.
Armed with poetry books by Robert Burns,
"Auld Lang Syne"* to Scotland changed not his stride.

An ocean apart, settled on a Wisconsin farm.
Botany class sent him flying to the woods.
Money scarce, he worked at a wagon shop.
With machines, his brain proved to be shrewd.

A sharp tool slipped and struck his eyes.
Six weeks confined to a darkened room.
Day or night he could not tell.
John of the Mountains met his doom.

The bitter woe turned out to be sweet.
Again, he saw the world in a new light.
God nearly killed him to teach a lesson.
Listen to conscience, true to his own sight.

Kentucky, Florida, Cuba, there he roamed,
wildest, least trodden roads he took.
In California, he found his true love in Yosemite.
Cliffs, waterfalls, a lifetime book.

John of the Mountains built a cabin near the creek.
For years, he listened to the river's talk.
A cup, a loaf of bread into the hinterland.
A copy of Emerson under the moon and nighthawk.

Bears, deer, bighorn sheep knew him well.
Precipice, rock face, mud and slough.
Glaciers to explore, mountains to climb.
He wrote and lived the life only he knew.

Ralph Waldo Emerson proclaimed him a prophet.
Sun shines in his eyes, stars twinkle in his dream.
The Mountains are Calling**; leaves, trees talk to him.
Running water chatting through the meadow and stream.

God shined his destiny for these three nights.
Theodore Roosevelt came to town.
The President camped out alone with him.
John of the Mountains didn't let the world down.

The duo set off to camp in the back country.
By the campfire, they talked late into the night,
woke up in the snowfalls of Glacier Point.
Two great minds synced to do things right.

He insisted we hear nature's call.
The voices of his unashamed emotions.
He revered wild nature over human culture.
Confronted mankind's conceit with devotions.

John of the Mountains, saint of the wilderness.
The world will look back to his prime.
Forests, glaciers, mountains he rediscovered.
The way he changed how we see nature in our time.

*A song by Robert Burns.
**Subtitle of the book "The Mountains of California,"
by John Muir.

127

Paradise *

When you were a little painter,
every line, color, came from me;
floating not on any foundation,
time and time again,
you saw me through the clouds.

When you were not a painter,
you forgot me.
You needed something solid
to sit on or stand up.

When you pick up brush again,
you try to paint me,
but cannot find me.
You think
you can reconstruct from your memory;
a river, trees full of foliage,
abundant fruits,
a bungalow, couple of hammocks...

But you cannot remember the color,
or how it floated.

*Published in *Chronogram* magazine, July 2021.

Nobody
(For Emily Dickinson)

Like a hermit; house and backyard,
lifetime on your guard.
What a dreadful idea to be a bard,
how public, revealing every card.

Like tussock sedges dance in the bog,
swaying their heads as breezes blow,
listening to the songs of jumping frogs
in the livelong June's glow.

You wanted to be nobody.
You knew by publishing your poetry
you would become somebody,
a puppet in the puppetry.

We Must Learn to Die
(for Rainer Maria Rilke)

"We must learn to die,
and to die in the fullest
sense of the word."*
How to say goodbye?
Through day-to-day strife,

vivid memories in our veins
in the face of loss.
How to transform from pain?
One wide river to cross.

The blowing wind I hear today,
same as when I was born,
whatever it is he tries to say,
you'll hear it when I'm gone.

*From the operas "Ring Cycle," by Richard Wagner.

My Old, Old Home

I heard you today.
I heard many chatting voices;
years, decades throughout.

The small circular trail is gone,
cement gave way to green grass,
and you still talk about that swing next to the shed.

When you were here,
a piano near the corner,
lullaby in the air,
courtyard beyond the threshold, flower beds.
Olive tree dropping black fruits
almost all season long.
Intermittent sunlight glittering
through the dark olives,
white-veiled green leaves,
and impatiens hidden under;
red, pink, white, purple, violet, indigo...
waiting patiently,
looking for the first excuse to burst open
impatiently.

131

Impatiens thrived in the shade,
laughter, tears, teasing,
lingered.

Almost a lifetime has passed,
I have changed many faces,
they all came and left.
Now the voices I heard from your family
bring back those moments.

What you claimed you lost,
you did not,
still in your voices,
I heard.

You were all so innocent,
So happy, happy,
when you were here.

About the Author

This is Livingston Rossmoor's 19th book. As of this writing, he has written and published 16 poetry books. Livingston has also written 2 books of prose and poetry, 1 book of 13 short stories and composed 21 lyrics and melodies collected in 2 DVDs and 1 CD. His poems have appeared in numerous publications: local newspapers, magazines, newsletters and overseas publications.

In addition, Livingston's poems have been published in *The Lyric, Poetry Quarterly, Ibbetson Street, California Quarterly* (California State Poetry Society), *Time of Singing* poetry journal and *Chronogram* magazine. Many of his poems were selected as honorable mentions in the following contests: *Writer's Digest Annual Writing Competition* and *California State Poetry Society Annual Contest*. One poem was awarded 3rd place in the *Annual Poetry Contest for the Dancing Poetry Festival*.

Livingston received his MS degree from UC Riverside and MA degree at UC Berkeley. Among his 40-plus year entrepreneur career,* he devoted many decades to publishing. Livingston oversaw the production of 12 printed consumer magazines. He is currently an associate member of the Academy of American Poets and a member of the California State Poetry Society.

Livingston resides in California with his dear wife. He has 3 children and 8 grandchildren.

*Livingston worked two jobs for 15 years to launch and build his various ventures; he was the founder, Chairman and CEO of four corporations at different stages of his business career in four fields: Radiopharmaceutical manufacture, real estate, software (SaaS) and publishing.

EGW Publishing
(Since 1979)

www.livingstonrossmoor.com

138